ENCOURAGEMENT FROM

THE PSALMS

ENCOURAGEMENT FROM
THE PSALMS

A 40-DAY
DEVOTIONAL JOURNEY

PETER HORROBIN

Chosen

a division of Baker Publishing Group
Minneapolis, Minnesota

Published by Chosen Books
11400 Hampshire Avenue South
Bloomington, Minnesota 55438
www.chosenbooks.com

Chosen Books is a division of
Baker Publishing Group, Grand Rapids, Michigan

Printed in the United States of America

Library of Congress Cataloging-in-Publication Data
Names: Horrobin, Peter J. (Peter James), author.
Title: Encouragement from the Psalms : a 40-day devotional journey / Peter Horrobin.
Description: Minneapolis : Chosen, a division of Baker Publishing Group, 2019.
Identifiers: LCCN 2018053589| ISBN 9780800799410 (trade paper : alk. paper) | ISBN
    9781493419005 (e-book)
Subjects: LCSH: Bible. Psalms—Meditations.
Classification: LCC BS1430.54 .H67 2019 | DDC 242/.5—dc23
LC record available at https://lccn.loc.gov/2018053589

Cover design by Studio Gearbox

19 20 21 22 23 24 25   7 6 5 4 3 2 1

CONTENTS

INTRODUCTION

Whenever I am in need of personal encouragement, I turn to the psalms. They are a treasure chest of truth that feeds the spirit, builds up the soul and gives one the courage to press on with the business of life. The word *encouragement* means "giving someone support, confidence and hope"—and that is exactly what the psalms do.

There is a profound reason why throughout the history of God's people, for Jew and Gentile alike, reading (or singing!) the psalms has been a daily discipline wherever and whenever believers meet. The psalms provide the encouragement we all need, because they are founded on the reality of a personal walk with God, and they build faith.

The majority of the book of Psalms is written by David—an amazing man of God who, as a boy, learned not only to worship the Lord as he cared for his sheep, but also to trust in the Lord whenever he had a need, whether that need was spiritual, emotional, relational or even physical—when wild animals would attack his flock. God was his anchor in life; He was everything to David.

David had learned that whatever the situation, God was sufficient for his need. Something that would stand him in very good stead in many of the experiences of his remarkable life.

It is this childlike, but utterly manly, quality that God must have pointed out to Samuel when he came to anoint one of the sons of Jesse as the next king of Israel. As Samuel looked at each of the first seven sons in turn, his assumption was that one of these fine young men must be the future king that God had chosen.

But God had a different idea and said to Samuel, "Do not consider his appearance or his height, for I have rejected him. The LORD does not look at the things man looks at. Man looks at the outward appearance, but the LORD looks at the heart" (1 Samuel 16:7).

It was only when Samuel asked if Jesse had any other sons that the young boy, David, was brought from the hills, where he had been tending the sheep, to stand before Samuel. Then the Lord said to Samuel, "'Rise and anoint him; he is the one.' So Samuel took the horn of oil and anointed him in the presence of his brothers, and from that day on the Spirit of the LORD came upon David in power" (1 Samuel 16:12–13).

So when you read the psalms of David, not only are you reading the praise, worship and spiritual experiences of a boy who became a man after God's own heart, but you are reading the words of a man on whom the Spirit of the Lord rested. It is not surprising, therefore, that the psalms have been such a rich source of encouragement for God's people for more than three thousand years.

They will never become outdated, because they are the vibrant account of a relationship with the living God who never changes—He is the same yesterday, today and forever! And all the other psalms, written by others from the same period of history, are also hallmarked by God's inspiration and Spirit.

But the psalms are also hugely encouraging because they are not the worship songs of a man who never had any problems or who never made any mistakes. He pours out his heart to the Lord when his enemies attack or he is facing a day of trouble (see Psalm 27). And in spite of David's godliness, the earthiness of his humanity is evident throughout, perhaps no more so than in Psalm 51 when he is broken before the Lord following his adultery with Bathsheba and murder of Uriah. The psalms contain the essence of a man's relationship with God through all the ups and downs of life—they are food for the soul and living water for the spirit. There is meat and drink here for every circumstance of life.

So as you use this book as a devotional of encouragement, I pray that the reality of God's living presence will pervade your spirit and that you will learn to trust the Lord yet more in all the daily experiences of walking with God day by day. We live in a fallen world that is at enmity with the living God. But when we immerse ourselves in God's Word, He will lift up our heads and enable us to say with David: "The Lord is my light and my salvation—whom shall I fear?" (Psalm 27:1).

How to Use This Book

This book is laid out as a forty-step journey of faith. It is designed to be read little by little, one day at a time. Before you begin to read each day's Scripture and devotional reading, I encourage you to spend a few moments in prayer—lay aside all the concerns of the moment and ask the Holy Spirit to open up God's Word to you and to minister His truth into your inner being.

Then read the Scripture for the day—not once, but two or three times, allowing God to speak to you personally through the words from Scripture. Next, read the devotional with an open heart, asking God to show you how the things that are said can relate to events and circumstances in your own life. You may find it helpful to read the devotional through again.

At the end of each devotional is a suggested prayer that will help you anchor the daily truths into the reality of your own life. But I encourage you to pray more personally as well, applying whatever God has said to you through the devotional to your own situation.

Finally, there is a space for you to make your own personal comments about the Scripture and the devotional and keep a record of what God says to you. It has always been a huge encouragement to me to look back at the things that God has said or done in the past and track the record of God's hand on my life.

I pray that this little book will be a rich blessing to you, and that as you move on with God you will know His presence and empowering day by day.

Day 1

THE LORD IS *MY* SHEPHERD

The LORD is my shepherd, I shall not be in want. He makes me lie down in green pastures, he leads me beside quiet waters, he restores my soul. He guides me in paths of righteousness for his name's sake.

Psalm 23:1–3

There can be no more encouraging verses of Scripture with which to begin our devotional journey. Psalm 23 is the most well known of all the psalms for this very reason—it speaks of comfort and encouragement at every stage and in every condition of life.

God is unchangeable; He cannot ever change His character. His heart is that of a Shepherd for His people, and He longs to gather His sheep into His arms and speak to them words of comfort and blessing. Isaiah 40:11 tells us that "He tends his flock like a shepherd: He gathers the lambs in his arms and carries them close to his heart; he gently leads those that have young." This is the heart and character of our loving Creator God.

Then Jesus told the story of the shepherd who had a hundred sheep, but one of them had strayed and was lost—so he left the 99 who were safe and went seeking the lost sheep till he found it. And what joy there was when the sheep that was lost was restored to the flock (see Luke 15:1–7)!

In all these Scriptures God is not really talking about sheep; He is talking about the people He loves and using sheep as a picture that anyone and everyone can understand, whatever age and whatever culture. It is a universal image that speaks to the very core of who we are as human beings. We all have a deep inner need of being loved, nurtured and cared for by our heavenly Father. And He is ready, willing and able!

Jesus came to show us what the Father is really like, so when He said, "I am the good shepherd" (John 10:14), He was telling us that this is how God cares for us. He then said, "I know my sheep and my sheep know me." He knows each and every one of us and understands our situations and needs.

There are seasons in life when we have different needs, according to the stage of the journey we are walking through. Sometimes we are in need of rest in the human equivalent of walking through green pastures or lying by still waters. At those times we can take in deeply of His loving provision while He restores our souls. He wants to reequip us for the road ahead.

Then He promises to lead us along paths of righteousness—and at that point we will need to exercise our free will and choose to follow in the direction that He is leading. Because He is a good Shepherd, He will not lead us in a direction that is contrary to His will and purpose for our lives. The heart of the message of these verses is that God can be trusted, so as we begin this forty-day journey of encouragement, let's commit ourselves right now to trust Him every step of the way.

Thank You, Lord, that You are not only a good Shepherd but also my Shepherd. Thank You for Your promise to lead me in paths of righteousness. I choose now to follow where You lead as I trust You afresh for every day of the rest of my life. In Jesus' name, Amen.

DAY 1

Day 2

HE IS WATCHING OVER YOU!

For the LORD watches over the way of the righteous, but the way of the wicked will perish.

Psalm 1:6

Today's Scripture is a strong word of encouragement for God's people. The psalmist is saying that if we choose to walk in God's ways, He promises to watch over us.

God can see us, of course, wherever we are and whatever we are doing, even when we wander off from the way of the Lord—for we cannot escape from either His presence or His knowledge of us. But the words here, translated as "watch over," mean much more than God seeing us or being aware of what we are doing. They contain within them a powerful promise of loving protection.

Consider this example. A beach is a wonderful place for children to enjoy playing in the sand. But it is also a place of potential danger from the sea, or even from other people on the beach. So not only do Mom and Dad see their children playing on a beach, but they also watch over them—meaning that they are constantly aware of all that is happening around their children, looking out for any potential threats and at all times in a state of readiness to move quickly to act in case of danger.

I am here today only because my dad was watching over me at the beach when I was a very young boy. I wandered off and fell into a deep sea-pool. But Dad was watching over me and stretched down beneath the surface of the water and pulled me out, before the next wave could carry me away.

This is a perfect picture of what it means to watch over. The parents see what is happening—but they do more. They see and also act if the children are getting into danger and need help. They are watching over their children.

God's promise to those who choose to walk in righteousness is that He will watch over us just like this. In the earlier verses of this psalm, we read that people who walk in His ways will be like a tree that is planted by a river—one that always has fresh sustenance from the water—and as a result produces wonderful fruit.

Fruitfulness is a sure test of real spirituality. To be fruitful we need to be drawing water from the River of Life. We do this by keeping in close fellowship with the Lord and choosing to walk in His ways. The choices we make have a direct effect on both our protection and our fruitfulness. Father God is a good gardener—He loves to watch over His fruit in each one of our lives—including yours.

Thank You, Lord, for the wonderful promises in Your Word. Help me always to make the right choices and walk in Your ways so that my life may be very fruitful and that I may know Your loving protection as You watch over me. In Jesus' name, Amen.

Day 3

THE SLEEP OF PEACE

Know that the LORD has set apart the godly for himself; the LORD will hear when I call to him. . . . I will lie down and sleep in peace, for you alone, O LORD, make me dwell in safety.

Psalm 4:3, 8

A godly person is someone who chooses to walk in the ways of the Lord—to pursue righteousness and right living, whatever the circumstances or whatever the personal cost. God sees the heart and rewards with His presence those whose hearts are after Him. As our Scripture encourages us today, He has set apart the godly for Himself.

In every circumstance of life, we naturally prefer to keep the company of those who think as we do, enjoy similar interests, have similar objectives in life and can be really trusted. We are glad to call such people true friends.

Scripture tells us that we are made in the image and likeness of God, so how we feel about relationships is simply a reflection of how God feels about relationship with us. God enjoys walking with those who think as He does, have similar objectives in life and can be really trusted. Abraham was like that. James tells us that "'Abraham believed God, and it was credited to him as righteousness,' and he was called God's friend" (James 2:23).

It is sometimes tempting to look around at the world, see the endless pleasures available to the godless and be tempted to be jealous. But in the inner being of the lost, there can only be loneliness, because they do not have the best companion there could ever be walking with them—the living God! As believers we are incredibly privileged to know that the Lord will hear the unspoken cries of our hearts and speak into our lives when we turn to Him.

God rejoices to keep fellowship with those who love Him and choose to walk with Him and delight in His ways. And as a companion, you can talk with Him and share your heart, knowing that He is utterly trustworthy and will keep your heart secure in the peace of God.

There is no torment in sleep for those who have the peace of God's presence in their hearts. So whatever the circumstances you may be going through in the ups and downs of life, you can know that you are secure in Him—not just for time, but for eternity as well. And that is something that no earthly pleasure can ever provide. So be encouraged.

Thank You, Lord, for Your promise to be with those who choose to walk in Your ways and to hear when they call upon You. Help me, Lord, never to stray into pathways that take me away from Your presence. In Jesus' name, Amen.

DAY 3

Day 4

STARGAZING

When I consider your heavens, the work of your fingers, the moon and the stars, which you have set in place, what is man that you are mindful of him, the son of man that you care for him?

Psalm 8:3–4

The witness of Scripture, from beginning to end, is that God was and is the Creator of all things. Secular humanism is desperate, however, to write God out of the script and to use science to prove that, in some extraordinary way, the whole of the universe accidentally created itself out of absolutely nothing—not only self-creating the matter of which the universe is made, but simultaneously creating the space in which all of God's creation exists!

This is as scientifically nonsensical as sitting in the middle of a field, waiting for an airport and a Boeing 747 to self-create so that you can jet off on your holidays! We can be confident that this will never happen. In just the same way, we can be confident that the universe was not an accident, and that as the psalmist contemplated the glories of the heavens, he was right in his assessment that the moon and the stars are the work of God's hands.

Our sun is 93 million miles away from planet earth. But out there in space is a star so big that its diameter is more than eight times the distance between earth and the sun. When I contemplate the vastness and the glory of the universe and then look at the sheer miracle of a caterpillar turning into a butterfly, I cannot help but praise my God, the Creator of all things.

When the psalmist sees the magnificence of God's creation, he is lost in the miraculous wonder of the fact that this amazing God is mindful of his individual existence and cares about him. It is hard for him to comprehend that almighty God, the Creator of all things, is aware of who he is and what he is doing.

But that is the reality of our God. He created all things, but it is mankind, made in His image and likeness, who is at the center of His heart. When we look up to the heavens and see the magnificence of the night sky, we can be hugely encouraged that the God who put the stars in space and holds them in His hands is the same God who put us on planet earth and sent His Son to show us how much He loves us.

When I look at the sky at night, I can be deeply moved by the truth that the God who made it all has His ears and eyes open to hear my prayers and watch over me. So be encouraged. In spite of our apparent insignificance when compared with the vastness of the universe, He is mindful of you, loves you and cares for you. You are special to Him.

Thank You, Lord, for Your amazing creation. I marvel at the fact that You, who made all things, are mindful of who I am and care about me. Thank You for Your wonderful love and extraordinary provision for me and all Your children. In Jesus' name, Amen.

DAY 4

Day 5

YOU WILL NOT BE DISAPPOINTED

O LORD, by your hand save me from such men, from men of this world whose reward is in this life. You still the hunger of those you cherish; their sons have plenty, and they store up wealth for their children. And I—in righteousness I will see your face; when I awake, I will be satisfied with seeing your likeness.

Psalm 17:14–15

It is sometimes hard to look upon the success of people who have turned their backs on God, lived their lives in unrighteousness and made earthly achievements and material possessions their aims in life—especially when you are going through hard times yourself! This was often the case for David.

But even though David wrestled, as we all do, with these underlying injustices of the present life, there was something much deeper in David's life that enabled him to be an overcomer, whatever the prevailing circumstances. In his heart he really knew what God was like. The nature and character of the God he loved, and who loved him, were so interwoven into David's life that he knew he would never be disappointed by God.

In verse 15, David turns his attention away from the present life, away from the fact that we are all sinners—all, not just those with evil intent in their hearts—and makes a remarkable prophetic declaration of faith. What David prophesied about seeing the face of God would only become possible because of the sacrifice of Jesus on the cross, His glorious resurrection and the fact that right now He has gone to prepare a place for all the redeemed of God (see John 14:1–4), including you and me.

David, a man who openly confessed his own sins, declared that *in righteousness* he would see the face of God. It is only with sin forgiven and the slate wiped clean that one day we will be clothed in righteousness divine. And in righteousness, we will see the face of God.

There are times in life when we look forward to something with great anticipation, but it turns out to be a disappointing letdown. The little David had experienced of God was such that he knew, in a way that was beyond human understanding, that when he saw God face-to-face, it would not be a disappointing letdown. He would be satisfied—which means full to overflowing—with the joy of the experience.

Sometimes people think of death as something to be feared. To those who know and love the Lord, death has no sting (see 1 Corinthians 15:54–58). It is the gateway to the clothing room of heaven where we experience firsthand the righteousness of Christ and enter the holy presence of the living God.

Human eye has not yet seen the glorious vision that will then be ours, but we do know that Jesus came to show us what the Father is like. We can know for sure, therefore, that we will be overflowing with joy. Yes, we will be satisfied. In fact, more than satisfied. And we will never tire of the experience.

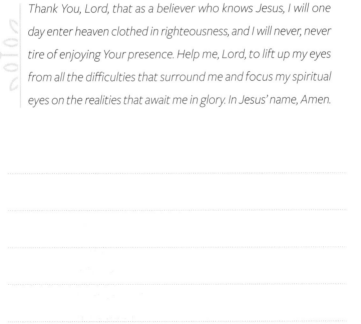

Thank You, Lord, that as a believer who knows Jesus, I will one day enter heaven clothed in righteousness, and I will never, never tire of enjoying Your presence. Help me, Lord, to lift up my eyes from all the difficulties that surround me and focus my spiritual eyes on the realities that await me in glory. In Jesus' name, Amen.

DAY 5

Day 6

MORE PRECIOUS THAN GOLD

The ordinances of the LORD are sure and altogether righteous. They are more precious than gold, than much pure gold; they are sweeter than honey, than honey from the comb. By them is your servant warned; in keeping them there is great reward.

Psalm 19:9–11

Gold is the international currency by which the governments of the world measure their worth. It is the ultimate trading commodity. Its value is determined by its qualities and its scarcity. A small amount of gold can be worth hundreds or even thousands of dollars.

Few of us own much of it, but what we do have we look after. We value it not only for its intrinsic worth in monetary terms but also for the additional value we give to it when we use it for special purposes such as wedding rings and fine jewelry.

But here the psalmist is telling us that there is something much more valuable than pure gold. And the Bible is not talking about even rarer metals or commodities such as platinum. It is referring to the simple life-changing and life-protecting truths that are contained within the Word of God and are available to each and every person absolutely free of charge.

For the fact is, if we choose to live our lives according to the Word of God, in obedience to the commands and ordinances of God, then we will be far richer than the worth of any valuables we might have stored away in the bank. And we will have greater wisdom than some of the most educated people on the planet.

I once prayed with a very rich and clever man; he owned the equivalent of much gold. But he had made some simple mistakes in life that meant that his riches were now of little significance to him, for he had lost a great deal in terms of family and relationships. What he had lost he wanted desperately, but what he had lost, no amount of money could buy. If only he had chosen to obey the commands of God, he would have discovered that they are worth much more than pure gold.

Earthly treasure can provide only earthly security; it is of no value in eternity. Jesus warned about focusing on our earthly wealth when He told the story of the man who decided to build bigger barns to store all his goods (see Luke 12:16–20). But, Jesus said, that night was to be his last on earth, and whom, then, would his treasure belong to?

God's heavenly treasure is available now through obedience to the teachings in His Word. What a blessing this will be to us in time—and then we will also enjoy God's reward in eternity! His eternal riches cannot be bought—even with gold. They are worth far more than all the gold in the world.

Thank You, Lord, that the blessings that come from walking in Your ways are of much greater value than pure gold. Help me, Lord, to avoid the plans of the enemy for my life and to treasure the blessings that come from obedience to Your ordinances. In Jesus' name, Amen.

DAY 6

Day 7

SHOW ME YOUR WAYS, LORD

*Show me your ways, O Lord, teach me your paths; guide me in your
truth and teach me, for you are God my Savior, and my hope is in
you all day long.*

Psalm 25:4–5

I visited the bridge of a ship recently and listened to the captain explain the intricacies of navigation. Ultimately, the safe passage of a ship depends not only on the navigators who plot her course through the seas, but also on the crew who act on the information supplied by the navigators. Obedience to the instructions is absolutely key for the safety of the vessel and for reaching the ship's expected destination.

In today's Scripture, we are encouraged to come to the Lord for His navigational instructions: We want to know what path He has set out before us for the next season of our lives. Without His guidance, we will always finish up a long way away from His best plan.

But, and this is a big *but*, if we know what the Lord would have us do and choose not to follow His navigational instructions, then we will soon be in trouble and make a shipwreck of our lives. After making an amazing transatlantic voyage in his ship, the *Santa Maria*, Christopher Columbus and his key crew members were exhausted and in need of sleep. They left the ship in charge of a young boy, but he did not follow his instructions. The ship foundered on a sandbank and was lost!

We cannot afford to let anyone other than the Lord be the navigator who shows us the direction we need to go. And we cannot allow anyone else to have control over our lives and take us to places God never intended. Learning always to trust Him and always to be obedient to His directions is the ultimate key to having the blessing of God on each and every area of our lives.

I love reading the biographies of the great Christian pioneers. It is enormously encouraging to see that when they pressed on with the things God had shown them to do, even against huge opposition and in great difficulty, the Lord blessed their work. Be encouraged that even when the going is tough, God will still navigate you through the high seas to achieve the destiny He puts before you.

If you take time daily to talk with God, to take in from the Word the truth of God and to listen in your spirit to the voice of God, you will find that He will lead you and direct your steps.

Thank You, Lord, that You rejoice to be the navigator of our lives. Help me, Lord, to take time daily not only to listen to Your voice but to obey Your instructions so that my life will fulfill the purposes that You planned for me. In Jesus' name, Amen.

DAY 7

Day 8

HEARING THE VOICE OF THE LORD

The Lord confides in those who fear him; he makes his covenant known to them. My eyes are ever on the Lord, for only he will release my feet from the snare.

Psalm 25:14–15

When you confide in someone, you are doing two things. First, you are trusting that person, and second, you are sharing with that person things you would not necessarily want anyone else to know. This remarkable verse expresses an incredible and amazing truth: that the living God, the Creator of the universe, wants to trust us and share with each one of us personally, in just this way!

He wants to share with us things that are precious and important to us, things that are not for anyone else to hear. But if we want to hear the Lord speak in this sort of way and share His heart with us, then there is a condition we need to fulfill. It is a very simple one: Have we learned to fear the Lord?

Fear the Lord does not mean to be afraid of Him because He is a frightening person. Rather, people who fear the Lord seek to walk in His ways because they love Him. Their first choice will always be to do those things that please Him. And it is to them that the Lord reveals the blessings that are to be enjoyed through understanding His covenant. Those who have the ear of the Lord will not need to be alarmed if they accidentally transgress His commandments, for they will constantly be aware of the Lord's gentle confiding voice showing them what is right and what is wrong, what is within His covenant provisions and what is not.

It is through this profound principle of covenant relationship with God that we are able to enjoy the guidance of the Lord in all of life's many different circumstances. I can think back to times when I chose not to listen to God's confiding voice and did my own thing—always those were proven to be bad decisions.

I learned the hard way that the only key to guidance that really matters is also the key to being in relationship with the Lord: enjoying life by living in holy fear of a holy God. Then the promise of the second part of the passage can be fulfilled. As our eyes are always on Him, the Lord will release us from snares laid on our pathway by the enemy of souls.

No wonder Isaiah said that the Sovereign Lord would come to "proclaim freedom for the captives" (Isaiah 61:1). There can be few things more encouraging than experiencing the leading of God guiding you so that you do not become ensnared by the enemy.

Lord, I would love to hear Your confiding voice as You share with me Your truths and lead me along the path of righteousness. Help me to desire above all else to walk day by day within the provisions of Your covenant blessings. In Jesus' name, Amen.

DAY 8

Day 9

WHEN WAITING IS SAFER THAN ACTING

I am still confident of this: I will see the goodness of the Lord in the land of the living. Wait for the Lord; be strong and take heart and wait for the Lord.

Psalm 27:13–14

David had many enemies and he faced many battles. At times he was on the run and situations seemed hopeless. But throughout all his trials and difficulties he never forgot the lessons of his early years. Lessons he had learned while looking after the sheep.

The Lord was close to him; he had learned to trust that inner voice of God, which had been his steadfast defense on so many occasions. God had shown him what to do when defending his flock from the lion and the bear.

When faced with the taunts of Goliath, God gave him the answer. And in times of battle God showed him exactly what to do, such as when facing attacks from the Philistines. Second Samuel 5:10 tells us that David "became more and more powerful, because the LORD God Almighty was with him."

David had learned that he really could trust the voice of his God. So David's words from today's Scripture are not just religious words without serious meaning; they were his own lifetime experience. He was passing on his experience of God to others and training them in the fact that even if things look pretty bleak, God can be trusted. It is better to wait for God to act than to act hastily and turn away from trusting Him.

Many years ago I was in the middle of a business crisis. I was under personal physical threat, and my business was on the edge of bankruptcy. It would have been easy to turn my back on God and blame Him for my problems, when in reality the mess was a result of my own mistake. But God heard my cry, and on the very day that my accuser began to threaten my very life, God delivered me from him in the most miraculous of ways. I felt like a bird that had been released from a trap. I was free. I could fly again. God had given me another chance.

I have never forgotten that experience. It is etched on my memory forever. I learned in the extremes of near disaster that to be strong and to wait for the Lord to act is not just good advice; on some occasions, it is lifesaving advice. Time and again I have taken huge encouragement from experiences such as this. But they have also been firm warnings not to ignore the voice of the Lord when He speaks caution into my heart.

Perhaps you are locked into a difficult situation with no obvious way out. May I encourage you to put your trust in the Lord, who delivered David on so many occasions out of the hand of his enemies? Never stop trusting the Lord. Wait patiently for Him to act.

Thank You, Lord, that You are a God who hears and answers prayer. Help me to be patient as I wait for You. I choose to trust You in a new way today, and I look forward to Your answer to the cries of my heart. In Jesus' name, Amen.

DAY 9

THE MERCY OF GOD

I will exalt you, O LORD, for you lifted me out of the depths and did not let my enemies gloat over me. O LORD my God, I called to you for help and you healed me. O LORD, you brought me up from the grave; you spared me from going down into the pit.

Psalm 30:1–3

David was an experienced warrior—but he was also experienced in the ways of God. From a young age, he had learned to worship and serve God. It was he, and not his older brothers, whom Samuel chose and anointed to be king. He had known God's protection and supernatural direction in difficult times on many occasions and had good reason to be thankful to God for His deliverance.

But Satan is always on the lookout for our weaknesses, and he knew David's Achilles' heel. He had the potential for being led astray by the sight of a beautiful woman—especially one who was bathing in the open air in a place that was visible from the palace roof. And we know how David fell into the trap. He not only committed adultery but finished up by having Bathsheba's husband killed to try to cover his sin.

But God in His mercy sent the prophet Nathan to confront David— at which point David had two choices: either humble himself, repent and call out to God for forgiveness and help, or use his authority as king to dispose of Nathan. At that point in his life he was either heading for the pit of destruction or the path of restoration. He made the right choice.

And God, in His mercy, heard David's cry, healed his broken heart and spared him from the consequences of his sin. What he had done could not be undone, but his relationship with God was restored. In walking the road of repentance, he was also climbing the hill of hope and putting his feet down firmly on the Rock of his salvation.

None of us is perfect, and the enemy will always be on the lookout for our weaknesses. But if we slip on our journey of faith and come face-to-face with the reality of our own sin, and if we react in the same way David did, then we will be assured of God's healing and restoration. Repentance and forgiveness are the double doors that open to the gateway of hope.

This is the heart of the Gospel—the encouraging Good News that God is merciful and forgiving. No matter what lies in your past or mine, when we come to the Father as did the Prodigal Son in Jesus' parable, then the Father runs to welcome us back and celebrates the restoration of the relationship. Good news indeed!

Thank You, Lord, that David knew the reality of Your healing and restoration. Help me, Lord, to follow You all my days. But if I do fall at any time, please show me, in Your mercy, so that I may follow David's example and know the joy of Your restoring love. In Jesus' name, Amen.

Day 11

DISCOVER THE TRUTH—
BY LEARNING TO TRUST

Taste and see that the Lord is good; blessed is the man who takes refuge in him. Fear the Lord, you his saints, for those who fear him lack nothing.

Psalm 34:8–9

Many years ago I was trained at a university as a scientist. My degree was in chemistry. Chemistry taught me to analyze carefully the substances I was working with and to test things out one step at a time.

Today's Scripture encourages us to have a similar approach to discovering the truth about God. When you taste something, you do not take a big mouthful and swallow it without thinking; you put a tiny bit on your tongue and test it. Then, if it tastes good, you eat it. And if there are no unwelcome side effects, you then remember that this particular food is good to eat. You need not test it anymore—you know what it is like.

I recently gave some of my favorite tropical fruit, papaya, to a friend. He had never tried papaya before. He tasted a small amount and discovered how good it is. He found that what I had told him about papaya was true. By trusting what I had said, he discovered the joys of soaking the papaya flesh with lemon juice, followed by a coating of sugar. He loved it.

One of the most encouraging steps I took in my own journey of faith was to discover that God's Word could be both tested and trusted. I learned that when we listen carefully to what God has said and then test it out in our own lives, He is faithful and true to His Word. I found that the things God has prepared for us are "good to eat," and that I can, therefore, depend on Him no matter what trials I face in life. Because God is trustworthy, His Word can also be trusted.

I was brought up on missionary stories, sometimes truly amazing ones, of how God had led people through difficult and testing circumstances. But it was not enough for me to hear the stories of what other people had done. I had to discover these things for myself by putting them into practice.

The joy of discovering that *their* God—the One who was everything to the central characters in those missionary stories—was also *my* God has been a source of encouragement throughout my life. I gain strength constantly from what God has done. It helps me press on to taste yet more of what the Lord has spread out on His table for me to eat.

The Lord has good things set out before each one of us. He will not force them upon us, but if we taste, we will see that what God has prepared is always good.

Help me, Lord, to trust what You say in Your Word—and then to apply it to my life. I do not want to discover the hard way that I have missed out on all Your blessings by not listening to what You say. In Jesus' name, Amen.

DAY 11

Day 12

BROKEN BUT LOVED

The LORD is close to the brokenhearted and saves those who are crushed in spirit.

Psalm 34:18

I once knew a man who always had eyes for those who were hurting. He would look out for people who were the "underdogs"—people who had little going for them in life and who had few natural advantages. He would come alongside them and make friends.

God had shown him that his mission in life was to be a friend to the people who had no friends, especially young people with their whole lives before them. The Lord showed him how to be generous to those who had very little of their own resources and to understand that these young people were just as precious to the Lord as the high achievers who had gotten it all together and were making a success of life.

Many of those young people were rescued from lives of rejection and inner pain by a man who believed in them and simply loved them into life. Where did he get such love?

There is only one possible source: The God who inspired the psalmist to write the words of today's Scripture was also at the center of this man's life. Jesus might not at this moment be walking the earth physically, but He is ever present in and through the lives of those who truly love Him—for if we really do love the Lord, then we will also really love those who, for whatever reason, are disadvantaged. Annie Flint's poem "The World's Bible," first published in 1918, sums this up so well:

> Christ has no hands but our hands, to do His work today;
> He has no feet but our feet, to lead men in His way;
> He has no tongue but our tongues, to tell men how He
>   died;
> He has no help but our help, to bring them to His side.

So when you read in the Word of God passages like this, about God being close to the brokenhearted, you can certainly rejoice. But do not forget that God may be asking you to be one of those who show the world what He is really like.

There is nothing more encouraging than sharing God's love with someone else and then seeing how your love becomes God's love in his or her heart. Derek Prince used to talk about being "God with skin on" for those who cross our paths in the daily activities of life.

Why not spend a few minutes looking back over your own life and thanking God for all those times when other people were "God with skin on" for you? And then accept the responsibility as a disciple to be "God with skin on" to whomever the Lord puts alongside you in life's journey.

Thank You, Lord, that You care about every single human being, and that all are equally precious to You. Forgive me for not being "God with skin on" for some of the people I have met. Open my eyes to see people with Your eyes and Your understanding and respond to them with Your love. In Jesus' name, Amen.

DAY 12

Day 13

THE FATHER'S DELIGHT

Delight yourself in the Lᴏʀᴅ and he will give you the desires of your heart.

Psalm 37:4

Don't you just love the promises of God! Like any good dad, He rejoices to bless His children. He wants them, whenever possible, to know and to enjoy His provision and blessing in their lives.

But there is a condition attached to the promise. It is a simple one: First delight yourself in Him.

Now what does that mean? First and foremost it means you must know Him and love Him. You cannot delight yourself in someone you do not like or love.

If you have an idea that God is not loveable, then you probably had some difficult experiences in life, especially when you were young, that make it hard for you to trust and love God. A father who never has time for his children, or one who is bad-tempered, selfish and angry, for example, can seriously influence how we think about God. And if we have any sense that this is what God is like, then it becomes almost impossible for us to delight ourselves in Him.

But be encouraged. If that, or anything like it, has been your experience, then you can look at Jesus, who came to show us what the Father is like. And then you can forgive those who have given you a wrong understanding of the nature of God, and ask Him to heal those memories and give you a fresh understanding of His love and His nature. God is able and willing to heal all of us, as we forgive those who have hurt us, so that we can freely express our love for Him.

Then, as is true when you really love someone, it becomes your joy and desire to find out what will bless that one. As you do this with God, you will discover that you are getting blessed yourself. You will find that there is a change in the things you desire. You are now looking for those things that will be a blessing to God in your relationship with Him. It is in this process that we discover an amazing dynamic taking place: The desires of our hearts have become the things that God wants to bless us with.

Yes, there are often tough times in life. But if our relationships with the Lord are right, He will sustain us through the tough times. We will discover the amazing truth that our desires, even then, become those that will bring joy to Father God. And those things that bring joy to Him are also the things that will bless us the most.

Thank You, Lord, for Your amazing love and that You delight to bless Your children. I choose, Lord, to delight myself in You. And then I trust You to give me the desires with which You fill my heart. In Jesus' name, Amen.

Day 14

HE LIFTED ME

I waited patiently for the Lord; he turned to me and heard my cry. He lifted me out of the slimy pit, out of the mud and mire; he set my feet on a rock and gave me a firm place to stand. He put a new song in my mouth, a hymn of praise to our God. Many will see and fear and put their trust in the Lord.

Psalm 40:1–3

Recently as I walked our dog along the towpath of our local canal, I watched a drama unfold before my very eyes. On the other side of the canal I noticed a cow stuck in the mud. It was deeply embedded in the mire, totally unable to move. Immediately, I set off to tell the farmer, but my desire to help was like a prayer to God when He says, "Before they call I will answer" (Isaiah 65:24). For I saw that the farmer was already on his way!

A tractor was coming across the field, heading straight for the stranded cow. No human effort alone could have gotten this large and heavy cow out of the mess she was in. So the farmer put a strong rope round the cow's neck and attached the other end to the front of his tractor. Then, reversing gently away, he pulled the cow out of the mire and settled her on safe ground. It was rough treatment, but for the cow it was salvation. The cow was muddy and exhausted, but she could now recover from her ordeal in safety.

As I watched the rescue, I was reminded of today's Scripture. The whole of the human race was sinking deep in the mire of sin. No human effort could lift humanity out of the mess. Because of the weight of its own sin, mankind was sinking deeper and deeper. It needed a Farmer with a "divine tractor" to come and take charge.

But instead of the Farmer putting the rope round our necks, it was Jesus who endured the "rough treatment" for us, so that our feet might once again be placed on a rock of certainty. When He rescued us, we were covered by the mud of the world. The cleansing flow of the blood of Jesus is all we need to be cleaned up and released back into living a new life with and for Him.

As I watched, the rescued cow struggled to her feet again and carried on grazing in the field. I realized that the muddy hole was still there; the cow would now have to be careful not to fall back in. The enemy of souls hates it when God's children are rescued, and, like the cow, we must constantly be on our guard not to fall back into the enemy's mud.

We have so much to thank God for. He lifted us from the mess of our own making and gave us back our lives. We have the most encouraging story in the world to tell. May there be many who will be amazed at what God has done in our lives and as a result choose to put their trust in Him.

Thank You, Lord, for the lessons You show us from our experiences in life. Thank You for rescuing me from the miry clay and for putting my feet on the rock. Help me to stay there, anchored by the security of Your love. In Jesus' name, Amen.

Day 15

FACING TOUGH TIMES

Why are you downcast, O my soul? Why so disturbed within me? Put your hope in God, for I will yet praise him, my Savior and my God.

Psalm 42:5–6

The times when we most need encouragement are generally those when everything around us seems to be getting out of control, and we are struggling with people or circumstances or both.

David, who was no stranger to tough times, had learned that one of the ways of rising above the circumstances was to talk to himself. No, not in any sense of being a little unbalanced. When his spirit knew that his soul was struggling, he would speak to his own soul. In today's Scripture, David's spirit is speaking to his soul and asking himself a question: "What's going on inside? What's happening with me?"

We all go through times when we cannot make sense of how we feel on the inside or understand the effect that difficult relationships or events are having on us. Many things can trip us up and distress us. At times like these we need to keep on reminding ourselves of the reality of God's faithfulness in the midst of the fallen world in which we all live. We have an enemy of souls who desires to do with us what he tried to do with Simon Peter—throw him off course by tempting him to deny Jesus.

David had proven God over many years; he knew that God was dependable and trustworthy. He would never have forgotten what God did when Goliath the Philistine challenged the men of Israel. And there were many times in battle when God showed him exactly what to do to avoid defeat by the enemies of God's people.

Yes, he knew that God could be trusted. So he spoke to his own soul and reminded himself of this: "Even though you are feeling down at the moment, and circumstances seem to be getting on top of you, lift up your chin! Look firmly ahead, knowing that however long or dark the valley, God is still with you, and you will yet praise Him."

Many times in my own walk with the Lord I have been tempted to be depressed by the circumstances. I have had to speak to my own soul, reminding myself of all that God has done in the past. "Be encouraged," I say. "He has been utterly faithful."

If your circumstances are currently difficult, remember that God has not changed. Hope in God, for you will yet praise Him, your help and your God.

I am grateful, Lord, for the memories of times when You have been so very present in my life. Help me, Lord, not to give in to inner feelings when circumstances are tough. I choose now to trust You, Lord, afresh—my help and my God. In Jesus' name, Amen.

DAY 15

Day 16

I WILL FEAR *NO* EVIL

Even though I walk through the valley of the shadow of death, I will fear no evil, for you are with me; your rod and your staff, they comfort me.

Psalm 23:4

We return now to the words of Psalm 23, for they embrace every stage and experience of life—seasons of peace and tranquility, times when we are facing enemies, and the time of life we will all have to go through one day, the valley of the shadow of death.

On numerous occasions my wife, Fiona, and I have had to accompany dear ones through their own valleys of the shadow of death—most of them older members of our ministry teams or families we know, who had reached the end of their days. But on one occasion a much younger man suffered a major heart attack and a few hours later went to be with the Lord.

In almost his last words, just before the heart attack, he expressed to Fiona the urgency in his spirit about the need for holiness and unity in the work of Ellel Ministries, in which I have served the Lord for most of my life. He knew the Lord was asking him to speak to the leaders about these critical issues. After delivering his message, he was struck only an hour or so later by the heart attack and was left helpless on the ground.

Even though he knew that what he was going through was very serious, there was no panic and no fear. He was totally at peace that the Lord was with him in his personal journey through the valley of the shadow of death. With his final words, he told Fiona that he felt like a baby being held safe in his Father's arms. He was comforted in his spirit by the presence of the Lord, who carried him to the safety of eternity. The powers of darkness had no say in the matter. Demonic fear was powerless to intervene. His death, when it came, was a supreme God-moment.

This is the testimony of the saints of God. The Lord is their comforter at their greatest moments of personal need. No wonder Paul referred to Him as "the God of all comfort, who comforts us in all our troubles" in 2 Corinthians 1:3–4. And in 1 Corinthians 15:54 Paul declared, "Death is swallowed up in victory" (ESV).

While no one looks forward to the moment of dying, it is so very encouraging to know that when our time comes we have nothing to fear from the forces of evil. We have a place to go to, which the good

Shepherd has prepared for each one of His sheep. The Gospel is such incredibly good and encouraging news!

Thank You, Lord, for Your incredible love and provision for each one of Your children. Thank You that I can look forward to all the rest of my days, knowing that when it is my turn to walk through the valley of the shadow of death, You will be there to comfort me and welcome me to my eternal home with You. In Jesus' name, Amen.

Day 17

BE STILL—IN THE MIDST OF UPROAR

"Be still, and know that I am God; I will be exalted among the nations, I will be exalted in the earth." The Lord Almighty is with us; the God of Jacob is our fortress.

Psalm 46:10–11

Those words *Be still, and know that I am God* are very well known and loved, but they are often quoted out of the context of Psalm 46 from which they come. We can easily forget what God was really trying to say to us through these comforting words. In context, they are even more encouraging than we might have imagined. For, it is in the midst of trouble, when we most need it, that God is saying we can enjoy the amazing peace of His presence with us day by day.

Psalm 46 begins by saying that "God is our refuge and strength, an ever-present help in trouble." Later, in verse 6, it talks about the nations being in uproar, with kingdoms falling. In fact, the more I read this psalm the more I realize how utterly relevant it is for the world in which we are now living. It seems as though we can never turn on the news without being confronted with world events that describe nations in jeopardy, political and social disturbances, violent attacks on innocent people, refugees fleeing danger, hunger or famine, financial systems in danger of collapse and distress on every side.

It is in exactly these sorts of circumstances that God is speaking to His people and telling us to be at peace—for nothing that is happening in the world is outside His knowledge or understanding. He is above all these things. It is He who is speaking into our hearts today, telling us not to be afraid but to trust in Him.

We can be sure that the day will come when He is exalted above all the nations; the truth about God will be manifest for all the world to see. In the midst of all these things we can be assured of His presence, His comfort and His encouragement. In Psalm 37:39–40 David puts it like this: "The salvation of the righteous comes from the LORD; he is their stronghold in time of trouble. The LORD helps them and delivers them."

In the eye of a storm there can be complete calm. In just the same way God wants to be right at the center of our lives. We can know His peace and the calmness of His presence even when things are in turmoil around us. It is as we keep our eyes firmly fixed on Him that encouragement flows from the heart of God to the heart of man— from His heart to yours. And encouragement gives us the courage to keep trusting, even when everything around us seems to be in disarray.

Thank You, Lord, that I can trust You whatever the circumstances are—either in the world or in my personal life. I choose now to let Your peace fill my heart and to be still before You. I give into Your hands, Lord, all my affairs and choose to trust You in everything and for everything all my days. In Jesus' name, Amen.

DAY 17

Day 18

THE TRAIN ARRIVING
AT PLATFORM . . .

*For [man] sees that even the wise die; the fool and the stupid alike
must perish and leave their wealth to others. Their graves are their
homes forever, their dwelling places to all generations, though they
called lands by their own names. Man in his pomp will not remain;
he is like the beasts that perish.*

Psalm 49:10–12 ESV

"Now that's a strange Scripture to use in a devotional book on *encouragement!*" I can hear you saying. And I agree.

But as I was reading through the psalms in the English Standard
Version, I was struck by the acute simplicity of the message of these
verses. It does not matter who we are—rich or poor, wise or stupid—we

are all no different from the beasts of the field, in that there is a limit on our physical life-spans.

There is nothing more certain than the fact that a day will come when our earthly lives will come to an end. You may even have something important named after you—many buildings, states, provinces and even countries bear the names of famous individuals. But not even that can make anyone live one day longer than God intends. It does absolutely nothing for anyone's longevity.

Our news headlines are often punctuated by the report that someone significant has died. I read the obituaries regularly in the *Daily Telegraph*, and very occasionally they mention someone I once met or knew. The news of someone passing away like this is a constant reminder of the truth of our Scripture.

It does not matter who you are—one day you will be a headline and then the rest of the world will move on without you. As my older brother lay dying in the hospital, he described death as waiting on the railway platform for your train to come down the line, stop, pick you up and take you on to your next destination. Believers know where that destination is and that they have nothing to fear about the journey from time to eternity.

The wonder of the Gospel is that, even though physical death is a certainty, those who are in Christ have already tasted eternal life. We know our destination. There cannot be a more encouraging message than this! Believers are already in Christ and with Christ. Because, as Jesus said, He has gone before to prepare a place for us, we can face the reality of death without any fear or anxiety.

We live in a world where wealth, reputation and what others think of us has become the preoccupation of prosperous humanity. We will all leave our earthly possessions behind. But the riches that are the possession of the believer are ours for time and eternity.

Let us rejoice in this amazing truth, which is at the heart of the Gospel, and spend some time in great thanksgiving. Jesus is alive forevermore and preparing a place for you and for me (see John 14:1–6).

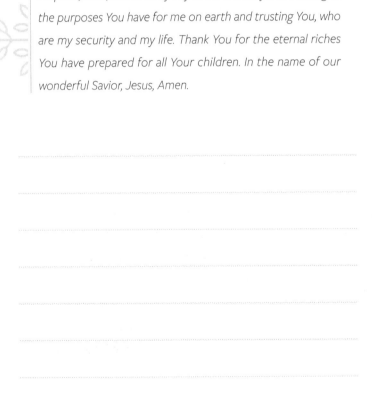

Help me, Lord, to live every day as if it were my last, fulfilling all the purposes You have for me on earth and trusting You, who are my security and my life. Thank You for the eternal riches You have prepared for all Your children. In the name of our wonderful Savior, Jesus, Amen.

Day 19

TRUST—THE ANTIDOTE TO FEAR

When I am afraid, I will trust in you. In God, whose word I praise, in God I trust; I will not be afraid.

Psalm 56:3–4

A new footbridge was recently opened in China. It is more than 1,400 feet long and spans a 980-foot-deep gorge. But it is different from other bridges: Its flooring is made of glass! Most people feel a natural reticence to trust a floor they cannot see. So in an opening display designed to give people confidence that the bridge is safe, officials drove a car full of passengers across it. There is no need to be afraid: If it will hold a car, it will hold you. The bridge is safe; you can trust it.

David, the psalmist, had learned in many difficult situations that God can be trusted. If God could enable him to kill Goliath with a stone from his sling and overcome the Philistines, then what reason did he have to be afraid of his enemies? God could surely be trusted in all situations.

We can look at hundreds of stories in the Scriptures in which God acted on behalf of His people and encouraged them in difficult or lonely situations. We can therefore say with confidence that this God, the God whom we love and serve, has demonstrated His trustworthiness in all aspects of life's journey.

I mentioned earlier that I was once faced with a dreadful situation in which a man motivated by evil was threatening my life. I will never forget the miraculous way in which God protected me. I know I can trust Him, therefore, to be my deliverer. I will never forget the miraculous way in which God provided the money with which we were able to purchase Ellel Grange back in 1986. I know I can trust Him to be my provider. And I cannot forget the hundreds, no, thousands, of times when in ministry situations God has set captives free and healed the brokenhearted.

If today you are struggling with personal fear, take courage from the many times in the Scriptures when God delivered His people. Think back to the times when God has been your personal help, healer or deliverer. Instead of letting the enemy grip your heart with fear, allow the Lord to surround your heart with love and the assurance of His presence in and through the journey of life that you are now on. He is utterly faithful and totally trustworthy. Be encouraged!

Thank You, Lord, that there is no situation in my life that You are unaware of. Whatever bridge You are asking me to cross, I know it is safe if You are with me. Help me, Lord, to overcome fear by walking hand in hand with You, in confidence that You are my deliverer, my provider and my healer. In Jesus' name, Amen.

DAY 19

Day 20

SHARING GOOD NEWS

Come and hear, all you who fear God, and I will tell what he has done for my soul.

Psalm 66:16 ESV

Reverence and awe are the primary constituents of holy fear. It is only those who revere God, and who worship Him in awe and wonder, whose ears are fully open to hear the voice of God and who know how much He rejoices in the testimony of a redeemed sinner.

To those whose ears are shut to the voice of God and whose eyes are closed to the creation of God, testimonies of salvation are no more meaningful than, say, giving scientific explanations of a nuclear reactor to an old man who never went to school. What would be meat and drink to the nuclear scientist would be indigestible nonsense to the individual uneducated in the sciences.

Until a person's understanding is opened to a knowledge of God and the reality of sin and its consequences, testimonies of salvation are received with obvious embarrassment and usually fall on deaf ears. But to those who have been saved, the stories of how God moved to give people new life—how they were born again and their souls saved from death and hell—are a source of intense joy and gladness.

Thus, it is those who already know the fear of the Lord whom the psalmist calls to come and hear his story. Throughout the psalms you can read about the goodness of the Lord. We read how God redeemed David after his catastrophic fall and restored him. We hear how God set his feet again upon a rock. And as we read these amazing songs of testimony, we are caught up in the joy and thanksgiving for all that God did for David's soul.

David could not stop telling God how grateful he was for His love and mercy. Psalm 66 ends with David saying (or singing), "Blessed be God, because he has not rejected my prayer or removed his steadfast love from me!" (ESV). Praise and thanksgiving build up one's spirit and bless those who fear the Lord. Why not spend a few minutes now rejoicing in all that God has done for you, and then share your testimony with great thanksgiving? Spend some time telling the Lord how wonderful He is.

And pray that when unbelievers see the fruit of your changed life, they will be prompted by the Spirit of God to ask the right questions. Then you can tell them that this is the fruit of what God has done for you. Once people start asking the right questions (as the woman at the well did in John 4), we then have the immense privilege of telling them the Good News.

I am so grateful, Lord, that You saved my soul and redeemed my life. Help me always to be thankful for Your goodness. And help me also, Lord, always to be willing to share the Good News with those who see the fruit of Your presence in my life and want to know more about You. In Jesus' name, Amen.

DAY 20

Day 21

WHEN GOD GOES DEAF!

If I had cherished sin in my heart, the Lord would not have listened.

Psalm 66:18

When I think about the word *cherish*, immediately I have a picture in my mind of showing love to someone I care about very much.

It came as something of a shock, therefore, to discover that the word *cherish* is here linked with something we are meant to hate: sin and its consequences. But the more I thought about it, the more I realized what an appropriate word it is to describe how we can sometimes think about things in our minds and dwell on them affectionately. In our thinking, we can imagine a great many things to do with the ideas we have.

There is nothing wrong with creative thinking, but we can think about both good and bad things. And when we dwell on the bad things, and cherish them in our hearts, we have crossed a line into ungodliness.

The writer of the letter to the Hebrews realized this all too well when he made it clear that, as far as God is concerned, the things we choose to dwell on in our minds can be as dangerous as the things we actually do. He explained that God judges the thoughts and attitudes of our hearts (see Hebrews 4:12). And we cannot overlook the words of Jesus when He told the crowd that looking on a woman to lust after her (dwelling on unclean things in one's mind) is seen by God as adultery and will be judged accordingly (see Matthew 5:28).

We need to seek God's help to be overcomers, not people who capitulate under pressure from the enemy to think ungodly things. One thing is absolutely certain: Satan listens very carefully to our ungodly thinking. It is not surprising, therefore, that so many people report that after an ungodly thought, they suddenly find themselves with the opportunity to put that ungodly thing into practice. The thought can open the door for the action.

Cherishing sinful things—dwelling on them in our minds because we love them—is clearly not something that blesses God. When the message God hears from our lips in prayer is saying one thing (we love Him), but the message God receives from our hearts is saying something quite different (we cherish sin), God will not be listening to those prayers. He has already turned His ear away from the message that is going heavenward from our hearts.

But be encouraged. This also means that when we cherish good and godly things in our hearts, God hears and rejoices to answer our prayers. This is one of the reasons why Paul, in Philippians 4:8, encourages us to think on good and lovely things. And then he concludes in verse 9 that "the God of peace will be with you."

May I encourage you to take some time to think about your thought life? Then ask God to help you deal with anything filling your imagination that would cause Him to turn a deaf ear.

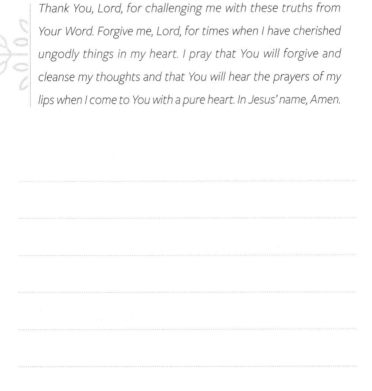

Thank You, Lord, for challenging me with these truths from Your Word. Forgive me, Lord, for times when I have cherished ungodly things in my heart. I pray that You will forgive and cleanse my thoughts and that You will hear the prayers of my lips when I come to You with a pure heart. In Jesus' name, Amen.

DAY 21

Day 22

LOOKING BACK WITH A THANKFUL HEART

*I will remember the deeds of the L*ORD*; yes, I will remember your miracles of long ago. I will meditate on all your works and consider all your mighty deeds.*

Psalm 77:11–12

When I was writing the story of how God first established the work of Ellel Ministries, at Ellel Grange in the U.K., I found myself thinking about the many things God did in those early days. As we stepped forward in faith, praying for those who came through the doors, looking to God for help, time and time again He intervened to bless and heal those in need, in spite of our lack of knowledge or experience.

We saw firsthand the miraculous power of God transforming people's lives. Looking back with thankfulness at what God did then has served to strengthen and renew my faith now for the days that lie ahead. We are living in increasingly tough times. We need to have landmarks of blessing to look back on with gratitude, and from which we can draw strength and inspiration.

I have realized afresh how meditating on what God has done in the past is such a wonderful source of encouragement for the future. For this reason, I read biographies of the saints of God—those inspiring stories of what God did through individuals who were willing to risk all in order to be obedient to what He was speaking into their lives. I have learned much through the experiences of others—just as we learn so much from the accounts of men and women of faith who fill the pages of our Bible.

I would like to encourage you to take time out to look back on your own life and write down all the things you can think of that God has done for you. Then meditate on each one, giving thanks to Him for the ways He has directed your steps.

It is also good to consider those things that have not gone so well because of your own wrong choices or disobedience and to come before God in repentance and ask Him for forgiveness. His Word says that He will forgive our sins and cleanse us from all unrighteousness (see 1 John 1:9). It is God's way of helping you to prepare a clean foundation for all that lies ahead.

People with thankful hearts are a joy to be with. May I also encourage you to share with others some of the things God has done so you can pass the joy around? You will, in turn, be an encouragement to them.

Thank You, Lord, for the amazing way in which You love to lead and direct our steps. I am so grateful, Lord, for all You have done for me. Forgive me, Lord, for the mistakes I have made, and help me prepare a new and restored foundation for all that lies ahead. In Jesus' name, Amen.

DAY 22

Day 23

THE JOURNEY BACK

Do not remember against us our former iniquities; let your compassion come speedily to meet us, for we are brought very low.

Psalm 79:8 ESV

When people turn their backs on God and walk away from His plans and purposes for their lives, there are consequences. Not because God is vindictive, but because He loves us so much. He wants us to be reminded of who He is and how much He loves us. Sometimes, when people run away deliberately and consistently from the place of God's blessing, they come to a position of being "brought very low" before they realize the true extent of what they have done.

In telling the parable of the Prodigal Son, Jesus used a very human story to teach profound spiritual principles. He was telling the people, first, about the consequences of running away from God and, second, in stark contrast to the mindset of the Pharisees, how the Father scans the horizon in order to lavish love on the son who was lost—not to reward his homecoming with punishment.

Being brought very low can sometimes be the essential first step in a long return journey, beginning with forgiveness and then eventual restoration to the place of sonship. This is the heart of God. But if we persist in being willfully rebellious, He cannot protect us from being brought very low. Unless we come face-to-face with the reality of where we are and what we are doing, we will never turn our hearts back to the Father.

It is sad to consider that, unless we face the truth about the rebellion in our hearts and turn back, we could fall to such a depth that we lose the blessings of fellowship with the Father in the timelessness of eternity (see Galatians 5:19–21).

Over the years, I have spent thousands of hours with people who were brought low and faced the brick wall caused by their own behavior. But what joy there is when they realize that this is the place where they have really met with the heart and character of a loving God, often for the first time! The Father envelopes them in His loving arms and lays out a feast of love to celebrate their return.

It is hard to watch people on a path that will inevitably lead to their being brought low. It can be easy to think that this is always the enemy's doing—and no doubt the enemy rejoices when people do hit rock bottom. But human desperation is God's opportunity. And whenever that happens it is time to rediscover the great love of Father God. That is the heart of healing. No one is beyond the love and the mercy of God. What a wonderfully encouraging truth!

Thank You, Lord, that even when I am brought very low, Your love for me never fails. And thank You for always scanning the horizon, looking for the moment when the lost turn again to You. Help me also, Lord, to be an agent of Your love and mercy to show others Your heart in their own times of need. In Jesus' name, Amen.

Day 24

GOD'S BLESSING
IN TOUGH TIMES

Blessed are those whose strength is in you [Lord], who have set their hearts on pilgrimage. As they pass through the Valley of Baca, they make it a place of springs; the autumn rains also cover it with pools. They go from strength to strength, till each appears before God in Zion.

Psalm 84:5–7

These three verses describe the journey of faith that believers often follow as they travel through life. A pilgrimage is not an occasional walk in the country; it is a determined commitment to keep on walking forward, until that moment when we step into the realms of glory and "each appears before God in Zion." The psalmist states without any hint of compromise that those who set their hearts on pilgrimage will be blessed.

But almost immediately the psalmist anchors this promise of blessing in the context of earthly reality. He recognizes that we are not exempt from the suffering hinted at by his reference to passing through the Valley of Baca. The word *Baca* means "a place of tears, or a place of weeping and lamentation." Tears are a godly expression of inner pain; they are also the first step on the road to comfort and healing. We are not, in this life, exempt from the possibility of suffering. This is illustrated graphically by Job's experiences, as described in the first chapter of his book.

Many events in life can be the source of pain and consequential tears. Perhaps the greatest suffering any of us can experience is the untimely loss of a loved one. Such events prompt unanswerable questions—questions that Jesus totally understands. To those in the midst of their pain of bereavement, Jesus Himself declared, "Blessed are those who mourn, for they will be comforted" (Matthew 5:4).

And, of course, Jesus also suffered the grief of bereavement when His cousin John the Baptist was beheaded. He understands our pain.

Today's Scripture then moves us on to the place of trusting God for the blessings that come from Him even in that place of tears—blessings that change the Valley of Baca into a place of springs that strengthen and equip us for the onward journey of faith and encourage us to keep walking forward.

In my own testimony, some of the most remarkable and blessed events have taken place in parallel with seasons of pain and suffering.

The Lord taught me from an early age to be determined in my obedience to Him, even when surrounding events could have tempted me to give up and turn aside from the road of faith.

My prayer for you, should you ever walk through your own personal Valley of Baca, is that in the midst of unanswerable questions, you will keep looking up to the Lord in faith, knowing that He is the only source of comfort and encouragement. Only He can touch the very core of your being and strengthen your heart for the pilgrimage ahead. The springs that well up in the valley will enable you to go from strength to strength.

Thank You, Lord, that You understand the hurts and pains I experience when traveling through my personal Valley of Baca. Help me today to keep on trusting You on the pilgrimage of faith, even when things happen that I cannot understand. In Jesus' name, Amen.

Day 25

THE WORK OF *YOUR* HANDS MATTERS

May the favor of the Lord our God rest upon us; establish the work of our hands for us—yes, establish the work of our hands.

Psalm 90:17

I sometimes hear people being so super-spiritual that it seems as though life on earth is of little importance to them: Their "real life" is going to be lived in heaven with God! As with many ways of thinking, this is both very true and very false.

Yes, in heaven we will be able to enjoy living in a way that is unprecedented here on earth, without any of the consequences of sin or human disappointment marring any aspect of life. And that is very encouraging. But if we think that our lives on earth are unimportant, then we have completely overlooked a very precious truth that is contained within Ephesians 2:10. Paul tells us that "we are God's workmanship, created in Christ Jesus to do good works, which God prepared in advance for us to do."

The things that God has prepared for each one of us to do are, indeed, precious—to us and to Him. The work of our hands is important to God. He is keenly interested in every aspect of our lives, and He rejoices in each one. It is right and proper to be praying that God will bless the work of our hands and establish—make firm and strong—whatever it is that we do.

God rejoiced when He created us and blessed us with gifts and abilities. He rejoices, therefore, in everything we do that fulfills His plans and purpose for our lives—and this means on earth, not just when we get to heaven. In the same way, human parents, who are made in the image and likeness of God, get terribly excited when their children start developing their own creative abilities. A rightfully proud parent will put the child's first painting on the wall, say how wonderful it is and rejoice at the offspring's achievement.

Once we understand that God is interested in us, in our work and in all the things we enjoy and do, then our attitude toward them changes. They are no longer an earthly drudgery but a divine appointment. They are no longer boring; they are thrilling. They are no longer a waste of time but a great opportunity.

It is in doing those things He has set before us, and in doing them well, that we prepare ourselves for seasons of blessing to come. We can know and be blessed by the favor of God—both here and in eternity. There is huge personal encouragement and deep inner joy awaiting us when we do those things God has made us for, using the gifts that He gave us.

Thank You, Lord, that You are interested in the works of my hands. Thank You for all the gifts and abilities You have given me. Help me always to seek to walk in Your ways, doing the things that please You all my days. In Jesus' name, Amen.

Day 26

TOUGH LOVE

Blessed is the man you discipline, O LORD, the man you teach from your law.

Psalm 94:12

Real love can be expressed in many ways. It is not loving *not* to warn a person who is in danger. And it is not loving to avoid giving a person correction when, without correction, he or she would be heading for trouble. On the face of it, receiving discipline might not feel encouraging, but without it the consequences could be disastrous.

I loved my dad—but I also had a healthy respect for him! He was incredibly loving and amazingly generous and fair, but he was also firm when it came to the point of bringing some needed correction into my life. I learned to recognize that Dad's love could sometimes hurt—at least for a season. But it was the sort of "hurt" that I knew was for my own good, even if I did not like it at the time.

A loving and disciplined environment made for an amazingly secure and safe family in which to grow up. I was very blessed. And even today I know I am being blessed by the straight edge of godly order that my dad helped establish in my life. Lessons learned well as a child are foundations for a lifetime, are never forgotten and should never be despised.

Now, if a human dad, who is not perfect and sometimes acts without full understanding, can be the source of such blessing, how much more can we expect our heavenly Dad to be a loving Father—a Father who has both perfect understanding and insight into our lives, and cares for us enough to want to teach us truth from His Word?

We may have to go through some tough times when we get it wrong, but a mature believer will welcome those times of discipline from the Lord. We can know for sure that God has no other objective but to bring us to a place of blessing. What He teaches us from His Word is *truth*. And when we choose to walk in His ways we will have *life*—abundant life and real blessing.

Hebrews 12:8 goes so far as to say that if we will not receive the discipline the Lord provides for us, then we are acting as illegitimate children and not true sons—for a true and loving Father will always seek to use discipline as a means of bringing godly order into our lives. The writer goes on to say that the discipline of God "produces a harvest of righteousness and peace for those who have been trained by it" (Hebrews 12:11). What a blessing!

Lord, I choose to welcome Your discipline in my life. Help me to see with Your eyes the things that need to change. I ask for the blessing of Your correction—now and always. In Jesus' name, Amen.

Day 27

KEEPING RECORDS
FOR FUTURE GENERATIONS

Let this be written for a future generation, that a people not yet created may praise the LORD.

Psalm 102:18

For some time now I have been gathering information about my family history and recording some of the things God has done in my life. I have an objective in mind that was inspired by today's Scripture. Children, grandchildren, nieces, nephews—the generations beyond will never have the opportunity to hear of all the things that God has done, and all the lessons I have learned in my walk with Him, unless I write them down.

Both my parents wrote out their own personal life stories, and reading how God led and provided for them has been an amazing blessing and encouragement to me. I am privileged to have most of the letters that my parents wrote to each other before they were married. When I read how they were already praying for their future children (meaning me and my brother!), I could not stop the tears of thanksgiving.

I know how interested I am in the pilgrimages through life of my parents, grandparents and ancestors. If, one day in the future, someone in my extended family should start asking questions about those who have gone before, I want the stories of what God did for previous generations to be available. Our experiences may even be the very means through which children yet to be born are drawn to wanting a personal faith in Jesus for themselves.

Remembering what God has done in the past is a theme that goes throughout Scripture. Both Moses and Joshua spent time reminding God's people about what He had done for them. Those stories continue to inspire, encourage and challenge the people of God to walk in His ways.

Some of the most powerful testimonies I have ever read were written by or about those who answered God's call to the mission field. Their life stories of commitment and sacrifice have inspired countless individuals to give themselves fully to God's call on their lives. They have been an enormous source of encouragement—especially for those going through tough times.

So when you experience the hand of God upon your life, may I encourage you to do what our Scripture says—write it down. Perhaps you do not have physical descendants, but remember that members of your wider family could be equally challenged, encouraged and blessed.

It is important to keep a record of the things God does. You never know how God might use your experiences of His faithfulness, guidance or provision. If the many personal stories—from Bible times up to the present day—had not been recorded, just imagine the huge amount of blessing we would miss.

And there is someone else who will benefit from your story: you! Think of the encouragement we receive from reading our own stories. When we recall the ways that God has led us in the past, these very lessons can give us the courage to press on to finish the race that God has set before us.

Thank You, Lord, for all the times You have blessed my life. Help me to remember these important lessons and write them down so that future generations will be able to read about what You have done for me. In Jesus' name, Amen.

Day 28

BEYOND COMPREHENSION

For as high as the heavens are above the earth, so great is his love for those who fear him; as far as the east is from the west, so far has he removed our transgressions from us.

Psalm 103:11–12

I think the psalmist could not have had any idea of the significance of what he was writing in these amazing words. He could see the stars in the sky, but he had no idea how far away they were and, much more significantly, no understanding of the infinite vastness of space beyond the visible stars. Perhaps, without realizing it, he was saying that there is no limit to the love of God.

Then consider the points of the compass. The North Pole and the South Pole are specific places on the surface of the earth. The distance between them is measurable. But not so the east and the west.

The distance between them cannot be calculated. What an incredible picture of what God in His love and mercy has done for us! When He forgives us, He removes our sins an immeasurable and infinite distance from us.

There is no limit to the love of God and no way for forgiven sins ever to catch up with us. God has dealt with them for all of time and all of eternity. I just love this amazing Gospel message, which is so dramatically illustrated by God's creation. Next time you look at the stars or fly above the world in a plane, take a few minutes to marvel at our amazing God.

Some people find it hard to believe that God actually loves them so much that He could ever forgive them. Some still carry the guilt and shame of things from the past where inner scars remain unhealed. Forgiveness deals with the eternal consequence of sin, but healing deals with the pain we carry in time—and we need both.

Without forgiveness we can never enjoy the intimacy of a personal relationship with God. And without healing we are in danger of carrying forward the pain of the past as a scar that will blight our future.

Receive the truth into your heart that there is no one who is outside the love of God. He longs to forgive and to heal so that we may truly live our lives in the encouragement of His love and the assurance of His presence.

For forgiveness, you need a repentant heart. For healing, you need to forgive all those who have hurt you and give God the inner pain that surrounds the issues of your past. And finally, you need to trust that

God is faithful to His Word. You are included in the *all* of the Gospel. Jesus died for your sins as well as everyone else's. What a faithful God we serve!

Thank You, Lord, for all You have done for me—for showing me such love and for dealing with my sin so comprehensively. You are amazing! In Jesus' name, Amen.

DAY 28

Day 29

GIVE THANKS— AND SPEAK IT OUT!

Give thanks to the Lord, for he is good; his love endures forever.
Let the redeemed of the Lord say this—those he redeemed from
the hand of the foe.

Psalm 107:1–2

I recently saw a most amazing piece of video, filmed in one of the game parks of South Africa. A young buffalo was attacked by a pride of lions on the edge of a watering hole. The lions were about to drag the baby buffalo away for a good meal when suddenly, out of the water, sprang a huge crocodile, which grabbed the other end of the baby buffalo!

At this point the young buffalo was being pulled in two directions— by a lion that had it by the head and by a crocodile that had its rear end!

It looked an impossible situation for the young buffalo. It was either going to be food for a crocodile or food for the lions.

But suddenly a whole herd of buffalo appeared on the edge of the watering hole. The emergency signal had gone out, and the buffaloes came running at a gallop to rescue one of their own. To see a large lion being tossed into the air on the horns of a buffalo was an amazing sight. The crocodile lost its grip and slid back into the water.

The young buffalo gave itself a shake and went off shielded on all sides by the herd. It was a totally extraordinary rescue act from what seemed an impossible situation.

As I watched that video I suddenly saw myself as that young buffalo, being targeted by all the powers of darkness who were wanting to pull me in all directions and rob me of my destiny, even my very life. Then over the horizon I saw my Redeemer, surrounded by the hosts of heaven, come to my rescue. He tossed the enemy (the roaring lion of 1 Peter 5:8) aside, and all the powers of darkness fled before Him. I saw myself being comforted by the angels as I walked away from the scene. I had been redeemed!

And I sure want to tell everyone what my Redeemer has done for me. I want to shout it out that the roaring lion has been defeated by the Lion of Judah, and that the crocodile, "Leviathan the gliding serpent . . . the monster of the sea" (Isaiah 27:1), has been defeated by my God. He redeemed me out of the jaws of death.

Yes, "let the redeemed of the Lord say so" (Psalm 107:2 ESV). Let's not be shy about celebrating the most amazing deliverance in the history of the world. The Lord rose in triumph, victorious over death and all the powers of darkness, and gave us the offer of new life. We have much to be encouraged by as we thank God for His amazing salvation and deliverance.

> *Thank You so much, Jesus, that You are my Redeemer—the one who rescued me from all the powers of darkness, from the roaring lions and from the leviathans that want to attack me. I am* **so** *grateful and want to tell the world what You have done for me. In Your name I pray, Amen.*

DAY 29

Day 30

MY LIFE IN HIS HANDS

This is the day the LORD has made; let us rejoice and be glad in it.

Psalm 118:24

There is fundamentally no difference between any of the days of the year. On each the sun will rise and the sun will set and the world's history will move forward by another 24 hours. But it is the passage of time that enables us to measure and record history. And every single day is a gift from the Lord, through which He wants to bless and encourage us.

Whenever we have extreme weather conditions, older people like myself start talking about what it was like in seasons past. When it is especially cold, for example, we talk about what it was like in 1947 or 1963—years when the snow and ice stayed on the ground for exceptionally long periods of time. I will never forget walking up the frozen river in Oxford and skating on the ice!

We put the memories of our own lives in place by remembering dates such as these, and we measure the events of history by what happened in, say, 1066, 1776 or, closer to home, 1914–1918 and 1939–1945. It is usually the traumatic events, such as the day when the Twin Towers fell in New York City in 2001, that are the most significant and memorable. For me as a student, it was the 1962 Cuban Missile Crisis—a standoff between Khrushchev and Kennedy that we all feared was going to end in nuclear war.

None of us knows what events might lie ahead of us. When we listen to or read the news we might be tempted to fear the unknown. But I have good news for you. While none of us knows the future, there is One who knows the end from the beginning. He is the only One who can be trusted to help you through whatever events and circumstances you may have to face. He is the only One who has your very best interests at heart and whose love for you is beyond measure or comprehension. And every day is one that He made.

It is a fact that as we trust Him in the present and act according to His will and leading, He determines our future. I want simply to trust the One who truly holds my life in His hands. I do not need to know what will happen tomorrow—for as long as I am trusting Him today I know my tomorrows are safe.

As we walk forward, trusting in the love and power of Almighty God, let's make every day a day of rejoicing and thanksgiving. Each one is a precious gift from our loving Creator. This day truly is a day that the Lord has made; let us rejoice and be glad in it.

Thank You, Lord, for every new day. Help me live each and every day knowing that You have made it and that, whatever happens, my times are utterly safe when they are committed into Your hands. In Jesus' name, Amen.

DAY 30

Day 31

EYE-OPENING TRUTHS

Open my eyes that I may see wonderful things in your law. I am a stranger on earth; do not hide your commands from me. My soul is consumed with longing for your laws at all times.

Psalm 119:18–20

I recently bought myself a new Bible. I was beginning to find the small print of my previous Bible something of a challenge when preaching—so the larger print version is a great help. But there was another reason also: My previous Bible is now so well marked I am sensing it is time to start again on a new adventure with God and His Word.

For me, getting a new Bible is scary. I wonder how I will cope without all the familiar and well-loved markings I read and use so often. But it is precisely the many markings that helped precipitate the change: These are the verses that draw my attention. I am in danger of missing precious truths contained in the unmarked verses!

So I am praying this wonderful prayer of the psalmist. I am asking God to open my eyes afresh. As I read my new Bible I want to understand yet more of the wonderful truths He has hidden in His Word.

We live in a fallen world, but it is into this world that God came—giving us both His written Word, the Bible, and the living Word, His Son, who became flesh (see John 1:1–5). With His written Word to guide us in the laws of God and the living Word to redeem us from the hand of the enemy, we are indeed a very privileged people. If only the leaders of our nations (and even God's people) were as consumed with wanting to know and live by the laws of God as the psalmist was!

As God's people, we should not want to be in tune with the ungodly objectives that consume so much of our fallen world. We are desperately in need of His revelation and truth. And it is here in God's Word that we can have daily revelation. We will never exhaust the knowledge of God that is available to us through His Word.

If this idea of reading your Bible with pen in hand is new to you, let me encourage you to try it. As you read, mark every line through which God speaks to you. In due course, as you browse through your Bible, the markings will be a constant source of encouragement.

And when your Bible is full of markings, get a new one. Then start again asking God each day for fresh understanding of His keys for your life.

The Holy Spirit who inspired the written Word is there to help you understand it. This has always been a massive encouragement to me in my Christian walk. I pray it will be for you also.

Help me, Lord, as I read Your Word, to have my spiritual eyes opened by Your Spirit. Help me see the things You have hidden there for my benefit and blessing and live according to Your laws. In Jesus' name, Amen.

DAY 31

Day 32

OBEYING GOD

I will always obey your law, for ever and ever. I will walk about in freedom, for I have sought out your precepts. I will speak of your statutes before kings and will not be put to shame, for I delight in your commands because I love them.

Psalm 119:44-47

For the past thirty years I have watched people come through the doors of Ellel Centers around the world on their way to healing retreats, training courses or conferences. Whatever the nationality or people group, the faces so often reveal a hard journey through life. Some of the battle scars picked up along the way are evident. It is sometimes clear that, for various reasons, these people have not been walking in freedom.

The whole of Psalm 119 is about the laws and the precepts of God—about how precious they are, about how when we follow them they give us wisdom beyond the intellect of man. In these remarkable verses from this, the longest psalm, the psalmist expresses a profound core truth: In obedience there is freedom.

This is a truth that lies at the heart of much of the healing people receive when they come in humility and submit their lives to the scrutiny of the Spirit of God, letting His Word and His truth be the arbiter of right or wrong in their lives.

Pride wants us to adjust the implications of Scripture to make it look as though we are never wrong. Humility recognizes that in our hearts there is a constant vulnerability to temptation. When we succumb to it, then we sin. And the fact is, sin has consequences. We cannot walk about in freedom when we have been bound by the consequences of our own ungodly choices—choices that are contrary to the laws and precepts of God.

Nothing gives me more joy than to see the changes in people's faces when they begin to walk about in the freedom that confession, forgiveness, deliverance and healing always bring. It is no wonder the psalmist came to the conclusion that there is nothing more sensible than to delight in obeying God's law. When we live within the limits of these provisions of God's mercy, then the enemy has no rights or grounds to enslave us in bondage—we are free! To walk about in such freedom is a totally liberating experience. It brings a smile to our faces, a spring to our steps—and makes our hearts rejoice.

Thank You, Lord, that in Your Word You have given us the keys to salvation. When I choose to walk in Your ways, then I will always know the freedom that only You can give. Help me, Lord, to remember Your laws and rejoice to walk in them forever and ever! In the name of Jesus, Amen.

Day 33

BE WISER THAN YOUR ENEMIES

Oh, how I love your law! I meditate on it all day long. Your commands make me wiser than my enemies, for they are ever with me.

Psalm 119:97–98

Wisdom and knowledge are very different. Two different people could look at exactly the same information and come to entirely different conclusions. The problem is this: Our understanding varies according to both our perspectives and our experiences.

We may think we know what a familiar mountain looks like, but when we see that same mountain from a different direction it looks entirely different. It is all a matter of our perspective. We may set out to climb the mountain a certain way only to discover it is impossible to approach the summit from that direction. The person with experience of having climbed the mountain before may set off in a direction that looks dubious, but he will get there first because he has learned from experience.

The problem with life is that we can look at all the circumstances prevailing around us and be at a loss as to the right thing to do. Our knowledge is limited, our perspective is not perfect and we have limited experience. What we lack is the wisdom to know what to do. We may have the facts, but we lack the understanding as to what to do with the facts.

But there is One who has all knowledge. His perspective on events and circumstances is always just right. The Lord is not limited by the horizons of our experience. On our journeys through life we need desperately to be taking our instructions from Him. This is why the psalmist was able to say, "Your commands make me wiser than my enemies." When we hear and obey His voice we will always be on solid ground.

God's wisdom is essential if we are going to make our way through this fallen world in which the enemy of souls is constantly working to drive us off course. With God's wisdom, we will always be wiser than our enemies. As we acknowledge Him, He will make our paths straight and show us the way to go—every step of the way.

It is always encouraging to start a journey through unknown territory with an experienced guide. Our guide for life is the Holy Spirit Himself, who makes the book of God alive with the reality of His presence and leading. We need not fear getting lost. He is there to direct our steps throughout life's journey, till that exciting day when we step from time into eternity.

Father God, I confess that many times I have depended on my own knowledge and experience and have not listened to Your voice or taken note of what You say in Your Word. Help me, Lord, to look up to You for the wisdom that passes all human understanding so that I will be wiser than my enemies and experience Your blessing on my path. In Jesus' name, Amen.

Day 34

LET ME LIVE

I long for your salvation, O Lᴏʀᴅ, and your law is my delight. Let me live that I may praise you, and may your laws sustain me. I have strayed like a lost sheep. Seek your servant, for I have not forgotten your commands.

Psalm 119:174–176

Over the last thirty years it has been a privilege to minister the healing love of God to people whose hearts are crying out to Him. They may not use the actual words of the psalmist, *Let me live*, but, in reality, that is what so many of them are saying.

For those who have been caught up in things that are ungodly, it is as if their very lives have been strangled out of them. They feel as though they are dying. They know the commands of God, but they have chosen to go their own way. They have, as the psalmist confessed for himself, "strayed like a lost sheep."

But the wonderful Good News is that Jesus came to seek and to save the lost sheep. He longs to bring them His healing and His salvation and restore their broken hearts. He longs to help them get their feet back on the right path. The desire of His heart is always to see His people fulfilled in their God-given destinies, rejoicing in who they are in God and safe in the knowledge that He has redeemed them from the clutches of the enemy.

When the psalmist cries out, "Let me live," he is expressing the desire of countless believers down the centuries who realize their predicament and see that they have nowhere else to turn. They have reached the end of the road and are desperate for a way out.

The fact is, sometimes we need to get to that point of desperation before our hearts turn and listen to what God might be saying. It is as if our spiritual ears are focused in the wrong direction—away from Him. Our physical ears are designed to collect the sound that is coming toward us. When we are walking away from people, it is hard to hear them. In just the same way, when we are walking away from God, we make it hard for our spiritual ears to hear what He is saying.

All we have to do is turn around, change direction. That is the heart of repentance. As soon as we start walking toward God, then things become clearer with every step we take. Our cry, "Let me live," is answered by the voice of the good Shepherd calling for His lost sheep.

Thank You, Jesus, that You love and care for us so much that You always look for the lost sheep—even me. Forgive me, Lord, for the times I missed Your voice because I was walking away from You. I choose to turn around and come running to the only One who can give me life. In Your name I pray, Amen.

Day 35

RETURNING WITH JOY

When the Lord brought back the captives to Zion, we were like men who dreamed. Our mouths were filled with laughter, our tongues with songs of joy. Then it was said among the nations, "The Lord has done great things for them." The Lord has done great things for us, and we are filled with joy.

Psalm 126:1–3

God's people had been exiled in a far country, under the control of a harsh regime. It is no wonder that when they were set free and returned home to Zion, the city of God, Jerusalem, they came back rejoicing. In their years of captivity they had thought about home, dreamed of being set free. When it actually happened, all their dreams came true.

For people who have suffered greatly, often through abuse, violence, trauma or misfortune, it can seem for them as though they have been living in a far country, limited by the boundaries and memories of the past as well as the sufferings that continue in the present. Day after day they look at other people without such limitations and dream of being free themselves. Their pain is ever in front of their eyes. In time, they begin to lose hope of having a normal life.

But in Isaiah 61:1–4, God paints a very different picture. He talks about those who are grieving and in mourning for what they have lost, those with broken hearts. He then speaks about Jesus through the prophet and declares that He will "proclaim freedom for the captives and release from darkness for the prisoners."

When you see a beautiful butterfly emerge from the encrusted exterior of a chrysalis, you marvel at the miracle of God's creative genius. In just the same way, when you see God bring healing to those who have suffered greatly, you marvel at the miracle of healing as another prisoner "returns to Zion" and rejoices in freedom from captivity.

The Lord truly does great things for those who come to Him with open and humble hearts. He longs, like the father of the Prodigal Son, to put His arms of love around them, to help them forgive those who have hurt them, to set them free from the work of the enemy and to give them back their joy. What a testimony it is in a world that has forgotten about God—to see the fruit of God's healing and restoring love in the life of one individual who has returned home in joy!

Joy is that uniquely Christian experience. It goes beyond the bounds of circumstantial happiness. Joy arises from a thankful heart and is expressed through all the different faculties that God has given us. It is like a bubbling stream that brings life and encouragement wherever it flows. May the joy the Lord brings be your encouragement today.

Thank You, Lord, for the great things You have done for me—and for the great things You continue to do in setting the captives free to love and serve You. In Jesus' name, Amen.

DAY 35

Day 36

SOWING THROUGH THE TEARS

Those who sow in tears will reap with songs of joy. He who goes out weeping, carrying seed to sow, will return with songs of joy, carrying sheaves with him.

Psalm 126:5–6

Life is not always easy. For some it is incredibly hard. Believers are not exempt from experiencing bad things. But how do we react when bad things happen? The psalmist is telling us that even through the darkest pain there can be songs of joy if we keep on sowing seeds of faith even as we struggle through the tears.

As I have prayed with people suffering from the consequences of traumas—traumas such as accidents, job loss, sickness, poverty, violence, premature death and even war—I see again and again that the circumstances are fresh in their minds. Unforgiveness in the heart is usually what keeps the wound fresh. It is a bit like creating a fresh bleed by picking at a scab before it is ready to drop off. The scab never heals.

Not long ago I looked at a gravestone in a country churchyard. I was impacted by the two names on the stone. They were brothers. Both of them were killed in action during the First World War. Their father was the minister of the church. I wonder how he coped with the double tragedy of having to bury both his sons, while at the same time declaring the glorious truths of the Gospel to his people? There is no doubt that many times in the rest of his ministry he would have been sowing through the tears.

Today's Scripture encourages us to keep on sowing, even through tears of pain or personal distress. It promises that those who keep on sowing with forgiving, thankful hearts will one day see the harvest. The tears of pain will become tears of joy at the harvest of souls.

It is not only the witness of our words that matters as we sow; it is also the witness of our lives. It is easy to be dynamic for God when everything is fine. It is quite another thing to maintain godliness in the face of crisis and pain. But it is the witness of our lives at times such as these that can have the greatest impact on the lives of others.

I know, for I have been impacted myself by the steadfast faith and witness of those who continued to sow seeds of loving encouragement into my life, while at the same time going through their own personal meltdowns.

How do you react when things go terribly wrong? Is it time to tell God you are sorry for allowing difficult circumstances to blunt the effectiveness of your Christian life and witness? Be encouraged. There are songs of joy to be sung as Jesus wipes away the tears and draws you to Himself.

Help me, Lord, not to carry the pain of bitterness by instead choosing to forgive. And then help me keep on sowing the good seed of the Kingdom, even when times are hard. Thank You, Jesus, that You did not give up when people turned against You. In Your name I pray, Amen.

Day 37

INNER BLESSINGS

How good and pleasant it is when brothers live together in unity! It is like precious oil poured on the head, running down on the beard, running down on Aaron's beard, down upon the collar of his robes. It is as if the dew of Hermon were falling on Mount Zion. For there the Lord bestows his blessing, even life forevermore.

Psalm 133

God always honors His promises. Through the promise of Psalm 133 He is teaching us a profound and life-changing principle. Not just a principle of unity and blessing through relationship with one another, but at an even deeper level. If we can truly understand this, it will transform the heart and open the door for the deepest possible inner healing and spiritual encouragement.

What am I talking about? I am referring to our own personal inner unity. We are made in the image and likeness of God. He is three-in-one: Father,

Son and Holy Spirit. Each human being is a reflection of our Creator in that we are also three-in-one: spirit, soul and body (see 1 Thessalonians 5:23).

Now Jesus said of His relationship with His Father that "I and the Father are one" (John 10:30). It is inconceivable that there could be any disunity in the Godhead.

For humankind things are different. Inner disunity is an outworking of the Fall. Here is what I mean. Because our spirits are cleansed in Jesus and brought into new life at salvation, our hearts can be genuinely intent on worshiping the Lord and doing His will. But at the same time we can be beset with temptation in the soul, and this can lead to sins of the flesh. Such disunity causes inner stress and strain and can even result in the body being vulnerable to physical maladies.

When we choose to bring our soulish choices under the headship of our spirits and discipline our bodies to obey, then we have inner unity of heart and purpose. At that point the peace of God transforms us from within. God is able to bestow upon us His blessing and His healing.

So, yes, our passage for today encourages us to know the blessing of unity that comes from being in a right relationship with our brothers and sisters. But if we are also experiencing the inner unity of spirit, soul and body, we will know the riches of God's inner blessings reaching to our innermost being.

It is this inner unity that creates the peace in our hearts that the world cannot give. It is truly beyond human understanding. But that does not make it any less real. It is the incredible privilege of being a child of God.

Let's not forget that when we are in disunity with those whom God has called us to love and serve, and when we are at disunity with ourselves, we experience something quite different from the blessings of God. In those situations we experience challenges that come from the inroads of the enemy into our lives and into our fellowships.

We have a choice to make—the blessing of God or the cursing of the enemy. I know what I want! How about you?

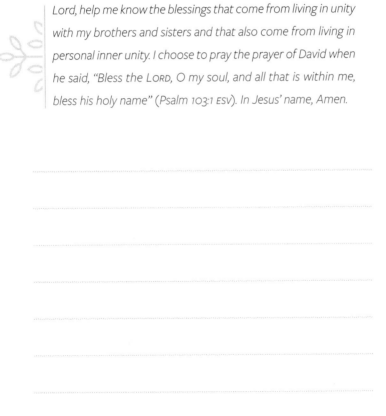

Lord, help me know the blessings that come from living in unity with my brothers and sisters and that also come from living in personal inner unity. I choose to pray the prayer of David when he said, "Bless the Lord, O my soul, and all that is within me, bless his holy name" (Psalm 103:1 ESV). In Jesus' name, Amen.

DAY 37

Day 38

GOD OUR RESCUER

*He who digs a hole and scoops it out falls into the pit he has made.
The trouble he causes recoils on himself; his violence comes down
on his own head.*

Psalm 7:15–16

Here is another Scripture that does not sound very encouraging! But
I want you to see that with God we can face the reality of our lives. He
will become an ever-present help in our day of trouble.

The other day I opened a newspaper and was transfixed by the pa-
thetically humorous picture of a young elephant that had fallen through
a drainage cover on a road in Thailand. The elephant was helpless, unable to move, trapped by its own weight and staring up its trunk with

a pair of huge eyes that simply said, "How did I get myself into this mess?" Don't worry—they got the elephant out!

But as I looked at the picture of the elephant that had fallen into the hole, it reminded me of many people I have known over the years who have done exactly what the psalmist was referring to. They have nurtured ungodliness in their life, often over a long period of time, until the weight of their ungodliness was too heavy for the flimsy spiritual ground on which they were standing.

The hole they were digging suddenly became a pit from which there was no way out. Everything had rebounded upon them; they had become victims of their own behavior. I stared at the picture of that helpless creature for quite a while and began to reexamine my own life. I realized afresh that there is no way any of us can get out of the pits we dig for ourselves.

But there is an answer! The way out, however, requires total honesty, full repentance and total dependence on the forgiveness and mercy of the God who sent His Son into the pit of sinful earth to rescue all those who look to Him for deliverance. It is only Jesus who can lift us out of such a pit and set our feet afresh on the Rock of our salvation. What extraordinary love our Savior has! We love Him because He first loved us.

So be encouraged. God is a specialist rescuer of those who have fallen into a pit of their own making. And no matter how deep the pit, His arms are long enough to reach everyone who cries out to Him for rescue.

Thank You, Jesus, for your extraordinary love—that even when we fall into the pits we have dug for ourselves, You long to come and set us free. Thank You that You never reject the broken and contrite hearts of those who look up to You from the pit with eyes of repentance, desperate for the forgiveness of their Savior and the security of His love. In Your name we pray, Amen.

DAY 38

Day 39

SEARCH AND RESCUE MISSION

Search me, O God, and know my heart; test me and know my anxious thoughts. See if there is any offensive way in me, and lead me in the way everlasting.

Psalm 139:23–24

It is not possible to look at ourselves with totally pure and objective hearts. Our motives are easily diverted from truth and reality. The natural instinct of fallen mankind is always to put a gloss on anything that is less than savory in our lives and pretend nothing is wrong. In order to know ourselves, therefore, we need help—and what better help could we get than that which David asked the Lord for?

God will always tell us the truth, however unpalatable it may be. It takes quite a lot of courage to pray this prayer of David with a totally open heart, when we realize that absolutely nothing is hidden from

God. We may find out some things about ourselves, and how we relate to others, that we would rather not know.

When, for example, we take offense over something, we break relationship with those who offended us. And when we break relationship, we lose the blessings that could be ours through those particular relationships. And when we wrongfully take offense against a fellow human being, we not only break relationship with that person but put a barrier between ourselves and God.

No wonder the psalmist was keen to ask the Lord to show him if there was anything in his behavior that had its root in offense. He did not want to be out of fellowship with the only one who could forgive sins. So he came before God with his whole life on open palms, and gave God full permission to share with him anything about himself that needed remedial attention.

David's prayer, which forms the Scripture for today, is one of the most profound, effective and encouraging prayers that anyone can ever pray. If we really mean the prayer, God *will* answer it. And as we listen carefully to the things He shows us, we have a wonderful opportunity for getting our lives back on track—not our track, but God's—His track for our lives.

I once passed a railway siding, a short stretch of sidetrack, on which hundreds of old and rusting railcars had been deposited. That speaks to me of the need to pray this prayer at regular intervals. None of us wants to wind up on one of life's sidetracks, rusting away and going nowhere. God has much more for us than that. When we truly pray the "search me" prayer, it can be the beginning of God's rescue mission for our lives.

Search me, O God, examine my heart, test my motives, show me my sins and help me know the things I cannot see for myself, so that I might change and be led by You in the way everlasting. In Jesus' name, Amen.

DAY 39

Day 40

ALL THE DAYS OF MY LIFE

You prepare a table before me in the presence of my enemies. You anoint my head with oil; my cup overflows. Surely goodness and love will follow me all the days of my life, and I will dwell in the house of the Lᴏʀᴅ forever.

Psalm 23:5–6

We have covered many topics in our devotional journey through the book of Psalms, looking at many different aspects of encouragement. For our final devotional, we return to Psalm 23, where we began.

All of us have a measure of time stretching ahead of us, but none of us knows exactly how much time we have. It could be days, weeks, months or many years. But however many or few those days are, the encouragement to live every day as if it were our last is sound spiritual advice. If we knew that today was the day in which we would be meeting the Lord face-to-face, we would not, under any circumstances, want to be involved in ungodly things. So why would we ever want to be involved in them?

The spiritual reality of daily life is that we are at all times living in a world that has sold its soul to the god of this world. We are, therefore, always in the midst of spiritual enemies. They are ultimately God's enemies, but because we are in Him, they are our enemies also. And this is one of the most encouraging Scriptures of all. Even in the midst of our enemies God is there for us. Or in the words of the psalmist, He prepares a table for us right there.

In my personal life and ministry, I have faced many different attacks and difficult circumstances. Perhaps you have, too. At all times God encourages us not to run away because of what the enemy might be doing, but to keep on pressing on with the calling and purposes He has for our lives. In the practical reality of daily Christian life, we can see how God has spread out provision for our needs, how He has anointed us for the work of our hands. I can say, and I hope you can, too, that my cup of thanksgiving overflows.

All that God has done is powerfully encouraging evidence that the One who was able in the past, and is able in the present, will always be there for us through our days on earth. And even better, we are assured that we will dwell with Him in the house of the Lord forever.

We always have a reason to give thanks. Consider with me Paul's advice:

Rejoice in the Lord always. . . . Do not be anxious about anything, but in everything, by prayer and petition, with thanksgiving, present your requests to God. And the peace of God, which transcends all understanding, will guard your hearts and your minds in Christ Jesus.

Philippians 4:4, 6–7

And let's finish our journey with these words from Psalm 100:

Enter his gates with thanksgiving and his courts with praise; give thanks to him and praise his name. For the LORD is good and his love endures forever; his faithfulness continues through all generations.

Psalm 100:4–5

A praising and thankful heart opens the door to a life of encouragement and blessing. I pray that will be your experience as you put your hand in His and walk together with Him.

Thank You, Lord, for the assurance of Your presence with me all my days and the promise of Your provision and encouragement every step of the way, until I can share in the joy, with You, of my eternal home with the saints of God. In Jesus' name, Amen.

Peter Horrobin is the founder and international director of Ellel Ministries International, which began in 1986 as a ministry of healing in the northwest of England. The work is now established in more than 35 different countries, providing teaching, training and personal ministry opportunities. The U.S.A. center is in Florida (www.ellel.org/USA).

After graduating from Oxford University with a degree in chemistry, Peter spent a number of years lecturing at the college and university level before leaving the academic environment for the world of business. Here he founded a series of successful publishing and bookselling companies.

In his twenties he started to restore a vintage sports car (an Alvis Speed 20) but discovered that its chassis was bent. As he looked at the broken vehicle, wondering if it could ever be repaired, he sensed God asking him a question: *You could restore this broken car, but I can restore broken lives. Which is more important?* It was obvious that broken lives were more important than broken cars, and so the beginning of a vision for healing and restoration was birthed in his heart.

A hallmark of Peter's ministry has been his willingness to step out in faith and see God move to fulfill His promises, often in remarkable ways. His book *Strands of Destiny* (Sovereign World, 2017) tells many of the amazing stories of what God has done in the past thirty years.

Peter has written many books, including *The Complete Catalogue of British Cars* (Morrow, 1974). And for the past 35 years he has been the editor of *Mission Praise* (Harper, 2015), one of the largest-selling hymn and songbooks in the U.K. and originally compiled for the visit of Billy Graham in 1984.

In this season of their lives, Peter and his wife, Fiona, are concentrating on writing so that all their knowledge and experience can be made permanently available in book form through publishers around the world. His book *Healing through Deliverance* (Chosen, 2008) is now a Christian classic.